Anglo-Indian Cookery

A selection of well-known dishes

by

Errol Anderson

www.angloindiancookery.com

Grosvenor House
Publishing Limited

This book is published by
Grosvenor House Publishing Ltd
28-30 High Street, Guildford, Surrey, GU1 3EL.
www.grosvenorhousepublishing.co.uk

A CIP record for this book
is available from the British Library

ISBN 978-1-78148-970-3

Dedicated to my mother Philo Anderson

Thank you. Without her support and patience, I would have never been able to compile this book.

Contents

ANGLO-INDIAN COOKERY

Introduction

The Anglo-Indian community is a distinct, small minority community originating in India. Anglo-Indian cuisine, dress, speech and religion all served to segregate Anglo-Indians from the native Indian population. Anglo-Indian cuisine is different from usual Indian recipes that you may have experienced. The Anglo-Indian cuisine developed over time where some English cuisine were enhanced by traditional Indian spices to give it a unique blend of culinary dishes which till date are prepared by Anglo-Indian families residing on all corners of the globe. The fusion food that emerged became a staple food of the Anglo-Indian community.

I emigrated from India to UK in 1989 leaving behind my parents. Few months after arriving here I felt home sick and most importantly I was missing the distinctive taste of Anglo-Indian home cooking. I struggled to comprehend with the common local cuisine when I have acquired taste of good Anglo-Indian food. At the time, although I enjoyed eating delicious food, I was novice to cooking. I started taking interest in cooking where I was helping out in the kitchen with basics like cooking rice and pepper water. A year later I moved out to stay on my own and it is only then I realized that I cannot rely on my minimalistic cooking skills and local food which was too bland for my liking.

In 1991 I went to India with the sole purpose of learning to cook especially Anglo-Indian Food. I had asked my mother to show me to cook most of my favorite dishes and I had also hired a professional cook to teach me some fine culinary skills which led me to cook my popular dish "Butter Chicken" I returned to the UK armed with knowledge of many good recipes and enhanced own cooking skills. It did not take me long before I started to show off my new found skills to my family and friends cooking for parties and functions.

My parents arrived in UK in 1993. My mother has always been known for her good culinary skills with having experience of cooking dishes passed down from my dad's mother who lived in Kolar Gold Fields (K.G.F), India and from my mother's mother who lived in Mangalore, India. I still have an old tattered recipe book where my dad kept note of all the good recipes.

Since the arrival of my mother here, my passion for cooking heightened which led me to believe that I should compile a book filled with recipes that have been passed down from generations, some from friends and relatives as well as including some of my own dishes developed over time. I would like to embrace the diversity of our food culture both past and present, emulating the fusion of great tasting Anglo-Indian recipes in this book.

My aim is to share these well-known recipes with people who have the willingness to try Anglo-Indian dishes and for them to experience cooking simple and tasteful dishes. The recipes are illustrated in an easy to read format for you to follow. You will notice that there are many common Indian spices been used in these recipes and hopefully the ingredients are accessible to you wherever you reside.

In majority of my dishes I have mentioned the use of pressure cooker especially to cook meat dishes. Using a pressure cooker will minimize the cooking time and will also make the meat tender and succulent. If you do not own one, it is worth investing as it can be used for both vegetarian and non-vegetarian cooking. As an alternative, you would need a good quality heavy-bottom medium to large saucepan.

Spices come in different forms, you can use them whole, ground, roasted, fried or mixed with yogurt to marinate meat and chicken. There are some fresh spices in the recipes like cinnamon, clove, green cardamom, where the spices need to be broiled, this can be obtained by placing the spices in a dry shallow saucepan and shaking the pan whilst it is broiling to stop them burning. By roasting the spices, they are easier to grind to powder. Spices will change the flavour of the dishes producing unique tastes and textures. The quantities of spices mentioned in this book is a guide, you can increase or decrease the quantity to suit your taste, especially chilli powder, mixed spices and salt. In most recipes I have use ground spices, which are generally available in supermarkets or Indian grocers. For grinding spices you could use a dry blender, food processor or my popular choice grinding spices using a pestle and mortar which really keeps the fragrance and texture fresh.

There are some of my recipes which requires the chicken to be made into tandoori pieces before being used to complete the dish. A tandoori oven is usually used in restaurant. The intense heat inside a tandoori oven make the chicken pieces crispy on the outside and whilst remaining tender and succulent inside. Cooking chicken in a tandoori oven brings out the best texture and flavor. The nearest you can get to the result of tandoori finish is by cooking the chicken pieces in a very hot oven or grill. When baking the chicken in the oven allow the water that come out of the chicken to remain until fully dried up so that the chicken pieces remain moist and succulent, if not, they will become really dry.

When cooking fries and curries, for best results the longer you cook over low heat, the better the taste of the food as it allows the spices to be absorbed. My suggestion would be to follow the recipe to the core in terms of ingredients, measurements and methods in order to obtain the same results expected from these recipes. However, you are most welcome to experiment with these recipes, as only you know how you want your food to taste. Hopefully, the photographs of the dishes included in this book will give you some idea of the expected results to work towards.

I hope that you will embrace my concept of sharing these recipes and join me in this journey of trying out all these wonderful recipes and bringing to your pallet these tasteful Anglo-Indian dishes.

I would like to take this opportunity to thank my mother, my wife Mary, relatives and friends who have helped me to realize my dream of penning a cookery book.

Happy Cooking!

Glossary

In general you can get most of the ingredients from good Indian grocer or super markets.

Ajwain seeds
Ajwain caraway or carom seeds are aromatic, less subtle in taste as well as slightly bitter and pungent.

Black Pepper
Round, black, hot flavoured seeds which can be used as whole or freshly ground, or as powder.

Bay Leaves
Dried leaves of the bay laurel tree, used in flavouring many dishes. You can substitute bay leaf for coriander leaves but will alter the flavour of the dish.

Black Cardamoms
Black skinned variety of cardamoms with strong fragrance used for flavouring curries and biryani.

Chana Dhal

It is a pale yellow colour lentils (chickpeas in half), which has a sweet nutty aroma. It is also known as Bengal gram (Gram Dhal).

Chilli (Green)

Fresh green chillies used as whole, slit and de-seeded gives the dish a pungent flavour.

Chilli (Red Dry)

Dried red chillies can be used as whole or crushed, can be substituted for chilli powder. Chilli gives colour, flavour and heat to most dishes. The quantity used in dishes can be altered depending on the hotness you require.

Cinnamon

Available as bark (cinnamon stick) or powder, an important curry spice, aromatic, warm and sweet in taste. A long cinnamon stick (15mm) equal to ¼ teaspoon of cinnamon powder.

Clove

Strongly aromatic and pungent curry spice, available as whole or powdered.

Coconut milk / Cream Coconut

Available in cans or add 250g fresh desiccated coconut to 500ml warm water. Blend to a smooth puree. Squeeze through muslin to collect the first milk. Repeat the process for second milk adding same amount of water until you are satisfied with the required quantity and consistency. Alternatively, you can dissolving cream coconut in water, 50g cream coconut to every ½ cup (125ml) water, depending on thickness required.

Coriander / Coriander Leaves

Available as coriander seeds whole or in powder form. This is an important curry spice which is used in most curries, it brings out a gentle fragrance which blends well with other curry spices to balance the dishes. Coriander leaves are used to garnish curries and fries to bring out its fragrance.

Cumin

This is an important curry spice that adds great taste to curries and fries, which has a warm pungent aromatic flavour. Available in powder form and seeds.

Curry Leaves

Pungent and aromatic leaves used in common Indian cuisine. They are usually available in bunches as sprigs.

Fennel Seeds

They look similar to the cumin seed but has a distinctive warm, sweet aroma and flavour. Available as dried seeds or powder.

Fenugreek seeds / Fenugreek Leaves

Used whole or ground in curries. Has a strong aroma, slightly bitter taste used for flavouring curries and pickles. Fenugreek leaves is available fresh and dried form, has a strong flavour and aroma often used in curries.

Garam Masala

A spice mixture that can be bought or
made at home

100g coriander seeds

60g cumin seeds

20g cardamom seeds

2 pieces of 1 inch (2.5 cm) cinnamon sticks

30g cloves

30g black peppercorns

½ tsp nutmeg powder

Broil all the spices first, then grind
and store in an airtight container.

ERROL ANDERSON

Garlic
White bulb separates into cloves. It is peeled then crushed to paste, pounded or chopped to add flavour to all types of food.

Ghee
Clarified butter can be substituted with cooking oil, butter or margarine.

Ginger
The root of a tropical plant, available fresh or powdered. Substitute ¼ teaspoon ginger powder for one thin slice of fresh ginger.

Green Cardamoms
Strong and aromatic curry spice, available as pods or powder. Two crushed cardamom pods is equal to ½ teaspoon of powder.

Lime Juice
Juice can be squeeze from fresh limes or purchased in bottles both as sweetened and unsweetened versions.

Mace
The outer skin of the nutmeg used as flavour to biryani and curries.

Mint
A refreshing, tangy fresh herb, a curry ingredient, used for biryani and for garnishing.

Mustard Seeds
Used whole or crushed in curries, has a strong, hot flavours. Often fried in oil to bring out their flavour before being combined with other ingredients.

Nutmeg
A pungent spice, available whole or in powder form.

ANGLO-INDIAN COOKERY

Onion

Onions chopped fine or sliced fine are fried until golden brown often used as the base for most curries and fries has a pungent taste and smell.

Rice

There are different varieties, usually served with curry or as a base for dishes such as biryani.

Star Anise

A dark brown anise-scented star shaped seed used in stew and curries.

Tamarind

Pods of a tamarind tree which has a sour taste, used to make tamarind water and add to curries for sourness.

Tandoori Paste

It is a blend of spices with tamarind, coriander and cumin used as a spice marinade for meat and vegetable alike. Also available in powder form.

Turmeric

A yellow fragrant spice extensively used to colour and flavour curries, vegetables and rice.

White Rice Flour

Flour produced from grinding polished rice. Can be used as a thickening agent for curries. Just add 1 tsp of white rice flour in 50ml warm water stirring vigorously, then empty this into the curry sauce and stir. Useful for thickening vindaloo curries.

Yeast

An agent for fermentation used in bread, cakes and wine.

Yoghurt

Fermented milk used as an ingredient in curries and for tenderizing the meat for fries. Often used in salads accompanied with onions, cucumber and coriander leaves.

Recipe guide

All the recipes are designed with an easy to follow step by step guide.

Ingredients

Most of the ingredients are listed in the order in which they are used.

Serving

Majority of the dishes are serving 4, with exceptions of a few which are 4-6, 6-8 and 8-10. This is because of the minimum required serving portion to achieve the best result.

Catering larger quantities

Most of the recipes can be doubled or even tripled and will still work well but you will need to take into account the quantity of hotness required as chilli powder will need to be reduced proportionately. For example, a dish that required 1 tsp chilli powder when other ingredients are doubled it should be 1 ½ tsp otherwise, the dish will be too chilli hot.

Timings

Preparation: This is based on the time taken to assemble the ingredients. Including chopping, peeling, slicing, blending, soaking. For example, slicing an onion, cutting garlic, ginger and crushing them to paste. Assumption are made here that most ingredients are at hand to start the preparation process.

Marinade: This depends on the minimum required time to ensure the ingredient is marinated well. However, this can be altered if you are time pressured but you may compromise on taste.

Active cooking: This is the amount of time you actually spend cooking the dish excluding baking time.

Total cooking: This is how long it would take from start to finish excluding preparation and marinating time. Basically from the time you start to cook the ingredients to actually finishing the dish.

All timings are based on approximation, depending on the utensils used, cooking expertise and appliances, which can slightly alter the taste and texture of the dish.

Conversion Tables

Dimensions	
Metric	Imperial
5mm	¼ inch
1cm	½ inch
2cm	¾ inch
2 ½cm	1inch
3cm	1¼ inch
4cm	1 ½ inch
4 ½cm	1 ¾ inch
5cm	2inch
6cm	2 ½ inch
7 ½cm	3inch
9cm	3 ½ inch
10cm	4inch
13cm	5inch
13 ½cm	5¼ inch
15cm	6inch
16cm	6 ½ inch
18cm	7inch
19cm	7 ½ inch
20cm	8inch
23cm	9inch
24cm	9 ½ inch
25 ½cm	10inch
28cm	11inch
30cm	12inch

Weights	
Metric	Imperial
10g	½oz
20g	¾oz
25g	1oz
40g	1 ½oz
50g	2oz
60g	2 ½oz
75g	3oz
110g	4oz
125g	4 ½oz
150g	5oz
175g	6oz
200g	7oz
225g	8oz
250g	9oz
350g	12oz
450g	1lb
700g	1lb 8oz
900g	2lb
1.35kg	3lb

Volume		
Metric	**Imperial**	**Other**
1 ½ml	0.05fl oz	¼ teaspoon
2 ½ml	0.09fl oz	½ teaspoon
5ml	0.18fl oz	1 teaspoon
20ml	0.70fl oz	1 tablespoon
55ml	2 fl oz	
75ml	3fl oz	
125ml	4fl oz	½ cup
150ml	5fl oz (¼ pint)	
250ml	9fl oz	1 cup
275ml	10fl oz (½ pint)	
570ml	1 pint	
725ml	1 ¼ pints	
1 litre	1 ¾ pints	
1 ½ litre	2 pints	
2 ¼ litre	4 pints	

Oven Temperatures			
Gas Mark	° C	° F	Other
1	140° C	275° F	Slow
2	150° C	300° F	Slow
3	170° C	325° F	Moderately slow
4	180° C	350° F	Moderately slow
5	190° C	375° F	Moderately
6	200° C	400° F	Moderately
7	220° C	425° F	Moderately hot
8	230° C	450° F	Moderately hot
9	240° C	475° F	Hot

Abbreviations	
tsp	teaspoon
tbsp	tablespoon
g	grams
kg	kilogramme
sprigs	A small shoot or twig of a plant

Soups

Usually soups are associated as a starter as it is in the western world. However, due to its spice content the soups here are rarely served as a starter instead they are prepared to accompany main course dishes like rice. Very seldom they are consumed on their own.

Bone Pepper Water

A traditional soup dish cooked with lamb bones and has an aroma of fenugreek.

20 minutes to prepare, 50 minutes cooking time

Serves 4-6

Ingredients

500g bones of lamb

3 tbsp oil

1 medium onion, finely chopped

3 green chillies, slit lengthwise

1 piece of I inch (2.5 cm) cinnamon stick

6 cloves

8 black peppercorns

2 tomatoes, chopped finely

50g cream coconut

1 tsp salt

½ tsp chilli powder

½ tsp ground turmeric

1 tsp ground cumin

1 ½ tsp ground coriander

1 tsp fresh garlic, crushed

1 tsp tamarind

2 tbsp roughly chopped coriander leaves

½ tsp whole mustard seeds

½ medium onion, finely chopped for frying

1 sprig of curry leaves

¼ tsp ground fenugreek

Method

1 Wash the bones and set aside.

2 Now put the bones, onions, green chillies, cinnamon, clove, black peppercorns, tomatoes, cream coconut, salt and boil in two cup of water in a large saucepan for 30 minutes.

3 Then add into the soup mixture chilli powder, turmeric, cumin, coriander, garlic, tamarind, coriander leaves and keep boiling for 10 minutes. Now remove from heat.

4 Heat oil in a shallow frying pan, add mustard seeds, after the mustard seeds start spluttering, add onions, curry leaves and fry for 1 minute. Now pour this over the soup and give it a light stir.

5 Finally, bring the soup again to boiling point, sprinkle with fenugreek and cook for a minute. Then remove from heat and cover the soup to preserve the fragrance.

Bone Pepper Water

Cook's Tip

You can use bones of beef but ensure the bones are cut into manageable size and cooked for little longer.

ANGLO-INDIAN COOKERY

Lamb Mulligatawny

An extremely good spicy soup made with lamb, dhal and curry spices. Served with rice or naan bread.

20 minutes to prepare, 50 minutes cooking time

Serves 4-6

Ingredients

500g lamb, washed and cut into small pieces

4 tbsp oil

3 tbsp gram dhal

½ tsp chilli powder

2 tsp ground coriander

1 tsp ground cumin

¼ tsp ground turmeric

1 tsp ground black pepper

¼ tsp ground clove

¼ tsp ground fenugreek

1 tsp whole mustard seeds

1 medium onion, finely chopped

1 sprig curry leaves

5 tsp fresh garlic, crushed

1 tsp fresh ginger root, crushed

1 ½ tsp Salt

500ml lamb stock

100ml thick coconut milk

1 large carrots, diced

1 potato, diced

2 tbsp roughly chopped coriander leaves

1 lemon, sliced

Method

1   Boil the gram dhal in two cups of water until soft and set aside.

2   Mix together chilli powder, ground coriander, cumin, turmeric, pepper, clove, fenugreek to smooth paste with 4 tbsp water and set aside.

3   Heat the oil in a large saucepan, add mustard seeds, after the mustard seeds start spluttering, add onions, curry leaves, ginger, garlic and cook until the onions are softened.

4   Add the mixed spices, the lamb and cook until lamb is browned, about 3 minutes.

5 Add salt, lamb stock, pressure cook on low the heat for about 15 minutes until the lamb is tender. Now open and add the coconut milk, carrots and potato and continue to pressure cook for further 5 minutes until the vegetables are soft.

6 Remove the lamb from the mixture and set aside. Now strain the contents and discard large pieces of residue left on the strainer including the curry leaves. Empty the liquid (soup) and the cooked gram with water into a blender, make it into fine paste.

7 Strain the soup through a fine mesh strainer or muslin cloth into another saucepan. Add the lamb to the strained soup, and cook until the soup is hot and ready to server.

8 Garnish with fresh coriander leaves and slice of lemon.

Cook's Tip

You can use beef or chicken.

Adjust the stock and cooking time.

Lamb Mulligatawny

ANGLO-INDIAN COOKERY

Pepper Water

A very pungent and spiced up water often compliments plain rice and can be consumed directly.

15 minutes to prepare, 25 minutes cooking time

Serves 4-6

Ingredients

3 tbsp oil

1 tsp black peppercorns

2 tsp whole cumin

2 dried chillies

6 cloves fresh garlic crushed

½ tsp mustard seeds

½ onion, finely chopped

2 sprigs curry leaves

¼ tsp ground turmeric

2 tomato, chopped

1 tsp tamarind

3 cups of water

2 tbsp roughly chopped coriander leaves

1 tsp salt

Method

1 Crush the black peppercorns, whole cumin, one dried chilli, garlic and keep aside (crushed Ingredients).

2 Heat oil in a medium size saucepan, when the oil is hot, put the mustard seeds.

3 After the mustard seeds start spluttering, add onions, curry leaves, one dried chilli cut into half and fry.

4 When the onion has browned add the crushed ingredients and stir.

5 Now mix turmeric, tomatoes and tamarind in water and squeeze them together. Now empty the squeezed contents including the water into the saucepan and add coriander leaves. Add salt to taste.

6 Bring it to the boil and remove from heat.

Pepper Water

Cook's Tip

Always use fresh curry leaves and coriander leaves for best result not dried leaves.

ANGLO-INDIAN COOKERY

Fries

The dishes in this section are described as fries meaning dishes are dry or semi-dry.

They are delectable accompaniments to main course dishes like rice.

There are some really mouth-watering and colourful dishes like pepper fry, lamb chops, pork roast which are among my favourites for entertaining guest. Dishes like chilli chicken, chilli salt fry and tandoori masala fry are great success at dinner parties and they are quite simple to cook.

Using freshly ground spices by broiling and grinding the spices will optimize the flavour of the dishes. Alternatively, using ground spices from supermarkets will suffice. The quantity of oil mentioned in the recipes are a rough guide and the oil used will depend on the size of the pan. In order to avoid burning the onions and other ingredients, it would be wise to fill the base of the pan with a thin layer of oil. You can vary the quantities of spices in these dishes to suit your taste.

Beef Chilli Salt Fry

The result is truly delicious. Compliments well as a side dish served with rice.

15 minutes to prepare, 30 minutes marinade time, 25-30 minutes cooking time

Serves 4-6

Ingredients

500g boneless beef, cut into thin slices

5 tbsp oil

400g canned tomatoes

¼ tsp ground turmeric

1 tsp chilli powder

1 tsp salt

2 large onions, sliced lengthwise

Method

1   Mix the beef, tomatoes, turmeric, chilli powder and salt in a bowl and marinate for half an hour.

2   Heat oil in a large saucepan or pressure cooker. Add the marinated mixture and 100ml of water. Cook on medium heat until the meat is tender.

3   Remove the lid and simmer until the water has evaporated.

4   Now add the onions and further cook until the onions are soft.

Beef Chilli Salt Fry

Cook's Tip

Slice the meat really thin to allow the meat to absorb the marinade and cook well. Adding the onions at the end brings out the flavour of the onions onto the meat. This dish gives the best flavour and texture when cooked with beef only.

Beef Crumb Chops

To begin with it is a long and delicate process but well worth it if you like your meat cooked like steak. There are different ways of finishing the dish but this one is my favourite.

25 minutes to prepare, 1 hour marinade time, 45-50 minutes cooking time

Serves 4-6

Ingredients

500g beef

3 tbsp oil

1 tsp ground black pepper

¼ tsp ground turmeric

2 tbsp vinegar

1 tsp salt

3 medium onions, finely chopped

2 green chillies, finely chopped

3 eggs

50g bread crumbs

Method

1 Cut the meat into thin pieces, wash and wipe them dry with a paper towel. Then tenderise the meat well.

2 Mix the meat with pepper, turmeric, vinegar, salt and marinade for an hour.

3 Mix the onion and green chillies in a bowl, then squeeze them to extract the juice and add this juice to the marinade.

4 Beat the eggs to fine consistency and keep aside.

5 Now squeeze the meat to make them dry.

6 Lay one flattened meat piece on your palm of your hand, place a small portion of the green chillies and onions mixture on the meat piece and then sprinkle the bread crumbs over it, pour a little egg on top to cover the mixture.

7 Heat oil in a shallow frying pan and place the mixture side down first and fry.

8 After 2 minutes, turn it over and fry for another 3 minutes on low heat (do not cover).

9 Repeat the process until all the meat pieces are cooked.

ANGLO-INDIAN COOKERY

Beef Crumb Chops

Cook's Tip

I have made this dish using chicken fillets and they do come out well but be warned it is quite a delicate process to keep the shape of the sliced chicken fillets throughout the process. Lamb is another alternative.

Beef Roast Fry

Instead of popping the roast joint into the oven, here you are cutting them into chunks and cooking them on the hob. This allows you to add the splendid Indian spices and for the meat to absorb the flavours. A great tasting dish and an ideal accompaniment to rice and curry dishes.

15 minutes to prepare, 30 minutes marinade time, 30 minutes cooking time
Serves 4-6

Ingredients

500g boneless beef

6 tbsp oil

4 long dry red chillies

10 cloves

15 black peppercorns

3 pieces of 1 inch (2.5 cm) cinnamon sticks

1 tsp salt

1 cup water

Method

1 Cut the beef in large chunks.

2 In a large saucepan or pressure cooker empty all the above ingredients including the beef, mix well and set aside for half an hour.

3 Switch on the heat and cook until the meat is tender.

4 Remove the lid and cook until the water has evaporated and the oil separates.

5 Switch off the heat and remove each cooked beef chunk and slice into thin pieces and return it back to the pan.

6 Switch on the heat and fry the meat until the meat is fully coated with roast oil. Switch off and the beef roast fry should be ready to serve.

ANGLO-INDIAN COOKERY

Beef Roast Fry

Cook's Tip

Ensure the beef chunks are cooked before slicing into thin pieces. Keep the roast oil when storing as the oil retains the flavour.

Cauliflower Fry

Prepared well the cauliflower should be soft inside and crispy outside. Makes a splendid accompaniment to a main dish.

10 minutes to prepare, 20-25 minutes cooking time

Serves 4

Ingredients

1 large cauliflower

Oil for deep frying

1 tsp chilli powder

¼ tsp ground turmeric

1 tsp salt

3 eggs

Method

1 Wash the cauliflower and drain off the water.

2 Separate the cauliflower into florets and wipe dry with a paper towel and keep aside.

3 Add the chilli powder, turmeric and salt in a bowl.

4 Now put the florets into the same bowl and mix well until fully coated.

5 Beat up the eggs and keep aside.

6 Dip the cauliflower pieces into the egg and deep fry for one minute until golden brown.

7 Remove the cooked florets one at a time, place on a plate with paper towel and allow for the oil to drain.

Cauliflower Fry

Cook's Tip

Give yourself ample time if you are particular on keeping the shape of each florets by separating them by hand. You can add more chilli powder if needed.

ERROL ANDERSON

Chilli Chicken

A really delicious dish.

15 minutes to prepare, 5 hours marinade time, 30-35 minutes cooking time

Serves 4-6

Ingredients

500g boneless chicken cut into small pieces

1 tsp fresh ginger root, crushed

3 tsp fresh garlic, crushed

1 tsp chilli powder

3 tbsp vinegar

¼ tsp red food colour

1 tsp salt

2 tbsp corn flour

3 eggs

Oil for deep frying

3 green chillies

1 sprig of curry leave

Method

1 Wash the chicken and pat dry with a paper towel.

2 Mix the ginger, garlic, chilli powder, vinegar, red food colour and salt with the chicken pieces. Mix until each chicken piece has blended well with the whole mixture.

3 Marinate the mixture and keep refrigerated for at least four hours or overnight.

4 Once marinated, add corn flour into the marinade and mix well.

5 Beat the eggs well, pour it into the marinated mixture and mix well.

6 Now keep aside the marinated mixture in cool dry place for an hour.

7 Heat the oil in a medium size deep saucepan and fry the chicken pieces a little at a time for approximately twelve minutes.

8 Repeat the process until all the chicken pieces are cooked.

9 You can garnish with fried green chillies and/or curry leaves.

ANGLO-INDIAN COOKERY

Chilli Chicken

Cook's Tip

For best result extend the marinade time allowing the spices to be absorbed well. Increase the quantity of chilli powder to the level of required hotness. Squeeze lemon over the chicken to add more flavour.

Fried Aubergine

Great accompaniment to rice dishes.

5 minutes to prepare, 15 minutes marinade time, 15-20 minutes cooking time

Serves 4-6

Ingredients

1 large aubergine

1 tsp chilli powder

½ tsp ground turmeric

½ tsp salt

½ tsp gram flour (optional)

3 tbsp oil for frying

Method

1   Thinly slice the aubergine breathwise and place in a large bowl.

2   Mix the chilli powder, turmeric, salt, gram flour with 3 tbsp of water in a bowl. Coat the aubergines in this mixture and set aside for 15 minutes.

3   In a shallow frying pan, heat oil, then add the aubergine few at a time, frying for a minute on each side until they are brown.

4   Remove the cooked aubergine and place on a plate.

Fried Aubergine

Cook's Tip

Alternatively, you can mix the spices in the bowl, then dip the aubergine and fry on both sides until brown. However, sprinkling the aubergine with salt and letting it rest removes the bitter juices, which would otherwise taint the flavour of the dish.

ERROL ANDERSON

Fried Fish

A simple dry dish with mild spices, the gram flour strengthens the fish crust, giving it a crispy finish.

15 minutes to prepare, 15 minutes marinade time, 25-30 minutes cooking time

Serves 4-6

Ingredients

8 fish fillets, cleaned

½ tsp fresh garlic, crushed

½ tsp fresh ginger root, crushed

½ tsp ground turmeric

1 ½ tsp chilli powder

½ tsp gram flour (optional)

1 tsp salt

4 tbsp oil for frying

1 lime, sliced in half

Method

1 Mix the fish fillets with all the above ingredients except lime and oil. Marinate for 15 minutes.

2 In a medium size shallow frying pan, heat oil and fry few pieces at a time and fry on both side until done.

3 Remove the cooked fish and place on a plate. Now squeeze the lime, spreading the juice over the fish.

Fried Fish

Cook's Tip

There is no real preference on the type of fish. Fry on low heat for best results.

Lamb Chops

A family favourite, which is easy to prepare. For best results ask your butcher to cut the lamb chops as thin as possible and marinate for longer period. Finishing with onions, potatoes and tomatoes makes this dish colourful and presentable.

15 minutes to prepare, 15 minutes marinade time, 35-40 minutes cooking time
Serves 4-6

Ingredients

500g Lamb back chops	2 tbsp vinegar
6 tbsp oil	1 ½ tsp salt
3 tsp fresh garlic, crushed	2 tbsp oil for shallow frying
1 tsp fresh ginger root, crushed	2 medium size potatoes
1 tsp chilli powder	2 medium onions, sliced lengthwise
¼ tsp ground turmeric	2 tomato, sliced round (breath wise)
2 tsp ground cumin	

Method

1 Wash the lamb and keep aside.
2 Mix garlic, ginger, chilli powder, turmeric, cumin, vinegar and 1 tsp salt with the lamb. Marinate for 15 minutes.
3 Heat the oil in a large saucepan or pressure cooker, empty the marinade and stir well. Add 100ml of water and cook until meat is tender.
4 Boil potatoes in a separate pot with ½ tsp salt and sufficient water. Once potatoes are boiled, peel skin off and cut it length-wise like potato wedges and shallow fry with 1 tbsp oil until golden brown, remove and keep aside.
5 Now fry the onions in a shallow frying pan with 1 tbsp oil, fry until golden brown and keep aside.
6 Slice the tomatoes and keep aside.

7 Mix the potato wedges, fried onions and tomatoes with the cooked lamb chops. Stir all the contents lightly just once.

Lamb Chops

Cook's Tip

Can be substituted with beef but may require to increase cooking time.

Lamb Pepper Fry

An exciting and tasty dish especially if you like the flavour of black peppers. Makes an impressive centrepiece for entertaining guest.

15 minutes to prepare, 45 minutes cooking time

Serves 4-6

Ingredients

500g boneless Lamb, cut into small cubes

6 tbsp oil

1 tsp ground black pepper

1 tsp salt

½ tsp ground turmeric

2 onions, sliced round (breath wise)

3 potatoes

2 tomatoes, sliced round (breath wise)

Method

1 Boil potatoes with sufficient water, peel skin off, cut potatoes like wedges and set aside.
2 Make oil hot in a large saucepan or pressure cooker, put in pepper and immediately put the meat, salt, turmeric and stir vigorously for few minutes.
3 Add one cup of water, cook for until meat is tender.
4 When the gravy is thick and the oil comes up, empty the onions and fry.
5 When the onions are soft, add the potato wedges and stir.
6 Then put the sliced tomatoes and stir gently just once and immediately remove from heat.

Lamb Pepper Fry

Cook's Tip

Beef or chicken can be used instead. Be really quick when putting the ground black pepper into the pan, add 1 tbsp of water if needed. You don't want to burn the pepper this will alter the taste of the dish.

Minced Meat Fry

This is a simple dish with a dry finish. Can be used as filler for bread sandwich, wraps and samosas.

15 minutes to prepare, 35 minutes cooking time

Serves 4-6

Ingredients

500g lean minced lamb

5 tbsp oil

1 medium onion, finely chopped

2 green chilli, chopped really fine

1 inch of fresh ginger, cleaned and minced

1 tsp chilli powder

2 tsp ground cumin

¼ tsp ground turmeric

200g canned tomatoes

1 ½ tsp salt

3 pieces of I inch (2.5 cm) cinnamon sticks

¼ tsp ground clove

2 tbsp roughly chopped coriander leaves

2 medium size potatoes cut into tiny cubes

Method

1 Heat the oil in a medium size saucepan.

2 Put the onions, green chilli and fry until golden brown.

3 Now add the ginger and fry for 30 seconds. Add chilli powder, cumin, turmeric and stir well.

4 Then add tomatoes and fry for two minutes.

5 Add minced meat, salt and stir well until the meat has blended with the Masala.

6 Now put cinnamon, clove and coriander leaves and add one cup (250ml) water. Cover and cook for ten minutes on medium heat.

7 Remove cover, add potatoes, 50ml water if required and then cover and cook for further ten minutes. Remove cover and cook until dry ensuring the potatoes do not get over cooked.

Minced Meat Fry

Cook's Tip

You can use beef mince, for best result ask your butcher to mince the meat twice.

Pork Roast Fry

Similar to the beef roast fry except you cut the pork into smaller pieces. A delightful and tasty dish making it a family favourite.

15 minutes to prepare, 30 minutes marinade time, 25-30 minutes cooking time

Serves 4-6

Ingredients

500g boneless pork

1 ½ tbsp vinegar

6 tbsp oil

4 long dry red chillies

7 cloves

7 black peppercorns

3 pieces of 1 inch (2.5 cm) cinnamon sticks

1 tsp salt

2 cups water

Method

1 Cut the pork into small pieces.

2 In a large saucepan or pressure cooker empty all the above ingredients including the pork, mix well and set aside for half an hour.

3 Now switch on the heat and cook until the meat is tender. Remove the lid and cook until the water has evaporated and the oil separates.

4 Fry the meat until the meat is fully coated with roast oil.

5 Switch off and the pork roast fry should be ready to serve.

ANGLO-INDIAN COOKERY

Pork Roast Fry

Cook's Tip

Cook on low heat ensuring that the pork does not overcook and remains tender.

ERROL ANDERSON

Spicy Chicken Fry

A dry spicy fry with strong fragrance of cinnamon.

15 minutes to prepare, 10 minutes marinade time, 30 minutes cooking time

Serves 4-6

Ingredients

500g chicken, skinned and cut into medium size pieces

6 tbsp oil

1 tsp chilli powder

2 tsp ground cumin powder

¼ tsp ground clove

¼ tsp ground turmeric

½ tsp ground cinnamon

1 tsp salt

200g canned tomatoes

Method

1 Wash the chicken and drain the water off.

2 Except oil, mix all the ingredients with the chicken and marinate for about ten minutes.

3 Heat oil in a medium size saucepan and put the marinade mixture and stir for two minutes.

4 Pour one cup of water, cover and cook for twenty minutes.

5 Remove the cover and cook until dry.

ANGLO-INDIAN COOKERY

Spicy Chicken Fry

Cook's Tip

Broil and grind the spices to give this dish more fragrance and a great taste.

 ERROL ANDERSON

Tandoori Masala Fry

Cooked tandoori chicken pieces finished with fennel seeds. A mouth-watering, aromatic and delicious dish.

15 minutes to prepare, 30 minutes marinade time, Oven 40 minutes, 30 minutes cooking time
Serves 6-8

Ingredients

1 kg chicken breast fillets

3 tbsp oil

2 tbsp yogurt

2 tsp tandoori curry paste

2 medium onions, finely chopped

1 tsp fresh ginger root, crushed

6 tsp fresh garlic, crushed

1 tsp chilli powder

3 tsp tandoori powder

200g canned tomatoes

1 tsp salt

2 tsp fennel seeds (pounded)

Method

1 Mix the chicken with yogurt, tandoori curry paste and marinate for 30 minutes.

2 Place the marinade in a baking tray and bake for forty minutes at gas mark 6, turning the chicken pieces every ten minutes until done. Once cooked, cut the chicken in small cubes and keep aside.

3 Heat the oil in a medium size saucepan, add the onions and cook until golden brown. Add the ginger, garlic and stir for a minute.

4 Then add chilli powder, tandoori powder and mix well for a further minute. Now add the tomatoes and stir.

5 Add the chicken pieces and sprinkle the salt over the chicken pieces.

6 Add the fennel seeds and stir well.

7 Cover and cook on low heat for four minutes. Open and dry for two minutes and the tandoori masala fry should be ready.

ANGLO-INDIAN COOKERY

Tandoori Masala Fry

Cook's Tip

When baking the tandoori chicken fillets keep the chicken fillets moist at all times retaining the water in the tray or sprinkle water if getting dry. Instead of freshly pounded fennel seeds you can use ground fennel reducing the quantity to 1 tsp.

Curries

In this section you will find a wide range for curries including pork, beef, lamb, chicken and fish.

Most of the recipes are well-known dishes like vindaloo and stew. There are some impressive centre piece for dinner party dishes like butter chicken, lamb korma and country captain chicken. The dumpling stew is an exceptional dish which is a main course on its own.

Making curries need not be tasking and gruesome, just requires a little patience and attention. The ingredients are listed in order of the steps mentioned under method to allow you to prepare your ingredients and follow them through step by step.

If the outcome of the curry dish turns out spicy you can add yoghurt or tomato juice to mellow the taste.

Curries are usually served with rice, chapattis or naan.

Butter Chicken

Cooked tandoori chicken pieces finished with fresh spices and cashew nut gravy. A superb mouth-watering dish that makes an impressive centerpiece for dinner party. Served with chapattis or naan bread.

20 minutes to prepare, marinade overnight, Active cooking time 50 minutes, Total cooking time 90 minute

Serves 8-10

Ingredients

1kg chicken breast fillets

150g tandoori curry paste or powder

100g yogurt

10 cloves

6 cardamoms

5 pieces of I inch (2.5 cm) cinnamon sticks

1 tsp ajwain seeds

½ tsp ground turmeric

1 tsp chilli powder

1 tsp ground cumin

200g cashew nuts

1 litre fresh milk

¼ tsp orange food colour

4 tbsp vegetable oil

2 tbsp ghee

6 medium onions, chopped fine

8 tsp fresh garlic, crushed

2 tsp fresh ginger root, crushed

2 green chillies, chopped fine

6 medium tomatoes, whipped to juice

2 tsp salt

Handful of dry fenugreek leaves, crushed

50g butter

2 tbsp roughly chopped coriander leaves

Preparation of tandoori chicken pieces

1 Marinate overnight the chicken breast with the tandoori powder or paste and yogurt.

2 Place the marinade in a baking tray and bake for forty minutes at gas mark 6 in the middle of the oven, turning the chicken breast fillets every ten minutes until done. Once cooked, cut the chicken in 1" cubes and keep aside.

Preparation of Spice mixture

1 Broil the cloves, cardamoms and cinnamon sticks in a frying pan and then grind them into fine power (ground spice mixture).
2 Then broil the ajwain seeds separately for few seconds, grind to powder and mix it with ground spice mixture.
3 Now add to the ground spice mixture turmeric, chilli powder, cumin and keep it aside (spicy mixture).

Preparation of the Gravy

1 Boil the cashew nuts in water until soft and strain the water off.
2 Then empty the cashew nuts and the milk into a mixer grinder and whip to fine paste. At this stage you can add a little food color and blend it for further minute (cashew nut mixture).

Cooking

1 In a large saucepan, heat the oil and ghee.
2 Now empty the onions, garlic, ginger and green chillies into the saucepan and stir well until the onions are slightly brown or when the oil starts to come up.
3 After the oil comes up, add the spice mixture and stir for a minute, then pour in the tomato juice and stir for few minutes (spice masala).
4 Now add the chicken pieces, sprinkle the salt over the chicken pieces and stir vigorously until every chicken piece is coated with the spice masala.
5 Now sprinkle the fenugreek leaves and continue stirring, cook for another minute and add the butter.
6 When nearly dry, add the cashew nut mixture and stir thoroughly. Cook for two minutes.
7 When the gravy starts to bubble, remove the saucepan from heat and garnish with fresh coriander leaves.

ANGLO-INDIAN COOKERY

Butter Chicken

Cook's Tip

If time constrained, you can reduce the marinating time to few hours. When reheating the dish, always add a little milk to avoid the gravy drying up.

Country Captain Chicken

This was the first fusion dish to be developed, making it part of the Anglo-Indian cuisine. A delicious mild stew with browned chicken pieces garnished with almonds and raisins. Served with rice.

15 minutes to prepare, 30 minutes marinade time, 35 minutes cooking time
Serves 4-6

Ingredients

1 whole chicken, cut into eight pieces

5 tbsp oil

2 garlic cloves, thinly sliced

1 tbsp fresh ginger root, crushed

½ tsp turmeric powder

2 cloves

1 tsp ground black pepper

½ tsp chilli powder

Juice of ½ lime

1 tsp salt

3 large onions sliced

2 fresh green chillies, chopped fine

2 bay leaves

½ cup unsalted chicken broth/ stock

1 handful of chopped fresh coriander to garnish

½ cup silver toasted almonds

½ cup currants or raisins

Method

1 In a bowl, put the chicken, garlic and ginger, turmeric, cloves, pepper and chilli powder, lime juice and salt. Mix well so the chicken is nicely coated. Keep aside for 30 minutes to marinate.

2 Heat oil in a large saucepan on medium heat and add the sliced onions, fry till they are golden brown.

3 Now add the green chillies, bay leaves and fry for a minute.

4 Add the marinated chicken and fry till the chicken has browned. Stir frequently to prevent the chicken from burning and sticking to the bottom of the saucepan.

5 Once browned, add the chicken broth/stock, cover and simmer on low heat for about 20 minutes until the chicken is tender and cooked. Remove the cover and cook until the gravy has thickened.

6 When the gravy has thickened, remove from the heat. Garnish with chopped coriander, almonds, raisins and serve.

Country Captain Chicken

Dumpling Stew

This is a superb stew with a distinctive taste created by the spices and dumplings. It is a main course on its own. It is one of those dishes that will certainly make one return for a second helpings.

20 minutes to prepare, 40 minutes cooking time

Serves 4-6

Ingredients

500g lamb cut into small pieces

3 pieces of I inch (2.5 cm) cinnamon sticks

6 cloves

8 whole black peppercorns

2 tsp salt

4 tbsp oil

1 medium onion, finely sliced

3 green chillies, slit lengthwise

¼ tsp turmeric powder

400g coarse rice flour

6 tbsp grated coconut

Method

1 In a pressure cooker, add two cups of water, lamb, cinnamon, cloves, black peppercorns, 1 tsp salt and cook until the meat is tender. Remove from heat and keep aside.

2 Heat oil in a large saucepan, fry the onions and green chillies until golden brown.

3 Empty the contents of the pressure cooker into the large saucepan, add three cups of water, add turmeric and cook on low heat.

4 In the meantime make the rice balls. In a bowl mix the rice flour with sufficient boiling water, 1 tsp salt, grated coconut and mix until it becomes a thick dough.

5 Now make walnut size balls, gently squeeze each rice ball with five fingers and keep it aside.

6 When the gravy is boiling, take the prepared rice balls and drop them in one by one. Cook for ten minutes until the rice balls are cooked.

Dumpling Stew

Cook's Tip

If preferred, you can add more grated coconut to increase the texture of the rice balls. However, this could make the rice balls heavier to digest.

ERROL ANDERSON

Egg Vindaloo

A hot and spicy egg curry usually served with rice.

15 minutes to prepare, 25-30 minutes cooking time

Serves 4-6

Ingredients

6-8 eggs (boiled, shelled and cut into halves using a twine)

5 tbsp oil

2 medium onions, finely chopped

1 tsp fresh ginger root, crushed

2 tsp fresh garlic, crushed

1 tsp chilli powder

2 tsp ground cumin

¼ tsp ground cinnamon

¼ tsp ground turmeric

1 tbsp vinegar

200g canned tomatoes

1 ½ tsp salt

Method

1 Heat the oil in a medium size saucepan, fry the onions, ginger and garlic until onions are golden brown.

2 Add the chilli powder, cumin, cinnamon, turmeric, vinegar and stir.

3 Add tomatoes, salt and fry until the oil separates.

4 Add 125ml water and bring to boil.

5 When the gravy has thickened add the hard boiled eggs and simmer for couple of minutes.

ANGLO-INDIAN COOKERY

Egg Vindaloo

Cook's Tip

If preferred, you can just score the eggs lightly rather the cutting them into halves, this will allow the eggs not to break up when serving.

ERROL ANDERSON

Fish Curry

A mild flavoured curry usually served with rice.

15 minutes to prepare, 25-30 minutes cooking time

Serves 4-6

Ingredients

500g fish fillets cut into medium pieces

5 tbsp oil

½ tsp mustard seeds

½ tsp fenugreek seeks

2 sprigs curry leaves

1 medium size onion, chopped finely

2 tbsp tamarind juice

1 ½ tsp salt

2 tbsp roughly chopped coriander leaves

For grinding the paste

1 tsp oil

1 medium size onion, chopped roughly

5 cloves of garlic, peeled

3 tbsp desiccated coconut

2 tsp chilli powder

½ tsp ground cumin

3 tsp ground coriander

¼ tsp ground turmeric

200g canned tomatoes

Method

1 In a shallow frying pan, add1 tsp oil, the roughly chopped onion, garlic and fry for a minute. Then add desiccated coconut, cumin, ground coriander, chilli powder, turmeric and stir fry on medium heat for a minute.

2 Empty the fried ingredients into a blender, then add the tomatoes, grind to a paste and keep aside.

ANGLO-INDIAN COOKERY

3 Heat oil in a medium size saucepan. Put the mustard seeds, when it splutters, add the fenugreek seeds and the curry leaves. Add the finely chopped onion and stir fry until golden brown.

4 Now add the ground mixture, tamarind juice and fry for about 3 minutes.

5 Add one cup of water and bring to a boil. Then add the fish pieces, salt and simmer for 2 minutes until the fish is cooked. Garnish with fresh coriander leaves.

Fish Curry

Fish Molee

A mild coconut flavoured curry usually served with rice.

15 minutes to prepare, 30 minutes marinade time, 40 minutes cooking time
Serves 4-6

Ingredients

3 tbsp oil

2 medium size onions, finely chopped

3 green chillies

2 tsp fresh ginger root, crushed

2 tsp fresh garlic, crushed

¼ tsp ground turmeric

1 tsp ground coriander

½ tsp ground black pepper

1 sprig curry leaves

1 tsp salt

200ml coconut milk

2 tbsp roughly chopped coriander leaves

For Marinating

500g fish fillets cut into medium pieces

1 tsp fresh garlic, crushed

1 tsp fresh ginger root, crushed

¼ tsp ground turmeric

½ tsp ground pepper

½ tsp salt

Method

1　Mix the fish with ginger, garlic, turmeric, pepper, salt and marinate for 30 minutes.

2　Heat oil in a shallow frying pan. Fry the marinated fish pieces for just 30 seconds, remove from heat and keep aside.

3　Heat oil in a medium size saucepan, add the onions and fry until golden brown.

4　Now add the green chillies, ginger, garlic, turmeric, ground coriander, pepper, curry leaves and fry for 30 seconds.

5　Add coconut milk, salt and simmer for 2 minutes.

6　Now add the cooked fish pieces and continue to simmer for further 2 minutes. Remove from heat and garnish with fresh coriander leaves.

Fish Molee

Cook's Tip

If preferred, you can use 100g cream coconut with 200ml water instead of coconut milk.

ERROL ANDERSON

63

Lamb and Aubergine Curry

A marvelous combination of lamb and aubergine resulting in a truly delicious dish, usually accompanied with rice.

15 minutes to prepare, 40 minutes cooking time

Serves 4-6

Ingredients

500g lamb

4 tbsp oil

2 medium onions, finely chopped fine

1 tsp fresh ginger root, crushed

2 tsp fresh garlic, crushed

1 tsp ground cumin

3 tsp ground coriander

1 tsp chilli powder

½ tsp ground turmeric

1 tomato chopped fine

50g cream coconut

2 tsp salt

12 small fresh aubergines

Method

1 Wash the aubergines, cut into pieces and immerse in water with pinch of salt and set aside.

2 Wash the meat and cut into small pieces and set aside.

3 Heat oil in a medium size saucepan and fry the onions until golden brown.

4 Add ginger, garlic, cumin, coriander, chilli powder, turmeric, tomatoes and stir well. When oil separates add the cream coconut and stir well.

5 Now add the meat, salt, add 200ml of water and stir well.

6 Cover and cook until meat is tender, now add the aubergines and cook until soft.

Lamb and Aubergine Curry

Lamb and Dhal Curry

A family favourite, the dhal mellows the spices to make the dish delectable to the pallet.

15 minutes to prepare, 40 minutes cooking time

Serves 4-6

Ingredients

500g lamb with bone

5 tbsp oil

½ cup chana dhal

1 sprig of curry leaves

1 medium onion, finely chopped

1 tsp fresh ginger root, crushed

1 tsp fresh garlic, crushed

1 tsp ground cumin

1 tsp chilli powder

2 tsp ground coriander

200g canned tomatoes

100g cream coconut

2 tsp salt

3 potatoes pealed and each cut into 4 pieces

Method

1   Cut the meat into small cubes and boil with three cups of water and 1 tsp salt until the meat is tender and keep aside.

2   In another medium size saucepan, boil the dhal with two cups of water, once the dhal is soft strain and keep aside.

3   In a large saucepan, heat the oil, fry the curry leaves and onions until golden brown.

4   Now add the ginger, garlic, cumin, chilli powder, coriander and fry.

5   Put the tomatoes and stir well. Add the cream coconut and stir well.

6   Now transfer the meat with the boiled water and dhal into the large saucepan, add 1 tsp salt and stir well.

7   Add the potatoes and cook on low heat until done.

Lamb and Dhal Curry

Lamb Korma

A mild creamy and delectable dish enhanced by the use of fresh spices and coconut. Served with rice or chapattis

15 minutes to prepare, 45 minutes cooking time

Serves 4-6

Ingredients

500g lamb, cut into small pieces

5 tbsp oil

1 tsp fresh ginger root, crushed

4 tsp fresh garlic, crushed

12 sprigs of fresh coriander leaves

2 green chillies

2 sprig curry leaves

1 medium onion, finely chopped

2 tsp ground coriander

1 tsp ground cumin

½ tsp ground cinnamon

¼ tsp ground clove

¼ ground turmeric

100g cream coconut

200g canned tomatoes

2 tsp salt

4 potatoes cut into 4 pieces

Method

1 Grind to paste the ginger, garlic, coriander leaves and green chillies (grounded paste).
2 Wash the lamb and drain the water off.
3 Heat the oil in a large saucepan/pressure cooker. Add the curry leaves, onions and fry until golden brown.
4 Add the grounded paste, ground coriander, cumin and fry until the oil separates. Add cinnamon, clove, turmeric, cream coconut and fry.
5 Now add the tomatoes and cook on slow fire.
6 Add the meat, salt and cook for three minutes. Now add three cups of water. Add the potatoes and cook until the lamb is tender and potatoes are done.

ANGLO-INDIAN COOKERY

Lamb Korma

Lamb Stew

A mildly spiced stew with a distinctive aroma of fresh spices.

15 minutes to prepare, 40 minutes cooking time

Serves 4-6

Ingredients

500g boned lamb

5 tbsp oil

2 sprig curry leaves

1 medium onion, finely chopped

1 long piece ginger, chopped into small pieces

4 cloves of garlic, chopped

4 green chillies, slit lengthwise

2 pieces of I inch (2.5 cm) cinnamon sticks

4 cloves

8 whole black peppercorn

¼ tsp ground turmeric

100g cream coconut

200g canned tomatoes

2 tsp salt

3 cups water

2 tbsp vinegar

Vegetables

2 medium size carrots, peeled and cut lengthwise 1 inch pieces

100g green peas

3 large potatoes peeled and cut into 4 pieces

¼ cabbage, chopped

Method

1 Wash the lamb and drain off the water. Cut the meat into 1 inch cubes.

2 Heat oil in a large sauce pan or pressure cooker, fry the curry leaves and onions until golden brown.

3 Add ginger, garlic, green chillies, cinnamon, cloves, black peppercorns, turmeric, cream coconut and fry.

4 Add the tomatoes and when the oil separates, add the meat, salt and water.

ANGLO-INDIAN COOKERY

5 Close and cook the meat for 8 minutes until the meat is tender, then open and add the vegetables. Add more water if required. Now close and cook for further 8 minutes. Open, add vinegar and mix well.

Lamb Stew

Cook's Tip

This sumptuous dish can go all wrong if you over cook the vegetables. Ensure the vegetables are not cut too small retaining their individuality. If preferred, you can substitute lamb for pork or beef. Also, you can use any seasonal vegetables of your choice.

ERROL ANDERSON

Minced Meat Ball Curry

A traditional family dish guaranteed to have been prepare in every Anglo-Indian home with mild variations. The spiced meat balls and the coconut gravy makes this a sumptuous and aromatic dish.

30 minutes to prepare, 30 minutes cooking time

Serves 6-8

Ingredients for the gravy

6 tbsp oil

1 Sprig curry leaves

2 large onions, finely chopped

1 tsp fresh ginger root, crushed

2 tsp fresh garlic, crushed

1 tsp chilli powder

1 tsp ground cumin

3 tsp ground coriander

½ tsp ground turmeric

½ tsp ground cinnamon

¼ tsp ground clove

1 ½ tsp salt

200g tomato juice

400ml coconut milk

2 cups water

4 medium size potatoes, each chopped into four pieces and boiled separately with a pinch of salt, strain the water and keep aside

2 tbsp roughly chopped coriander leaves for garnishing

ANGLO-INDIAN COOKERY

Ingredients for Meat balls

500g mince lamb or beef

1 medium onion, finely chopped

1 inch ginger finely chopped

2 green chillies, slit into half and finely chopped

2 tbsp finely chopped coriander leaves

½ tsp salt

2 tbsp of gravy from the curry mixture

Mix all the ingredients together for preparation of the minced meat balls, using the palm of your hands making balls of size of a walnut.

Method

1   Heat oil in a large saucepan and fry the curry leaves and onions until golden brown.

2   Now add ginger and garlic and stir. Then add chilli powder, cumin, ground coriander, turmeric, cinnamon, clove and fry for few minutes until the oil separates.

3   Now add tomatoes juice and fry for few minutes until the oil separates. Remove two tablespoons of this paste and add to the minced meat ball mixture.

4   Now add the coconut milk, water and simmer on low heat. In the meantime, start to prepare the minced meat balls.

5   When it starts to boil drop in the minced meat balls one by one ensuring they do not stick to each other.

6   After 10 minutes drop in the cooked potatoes and stir.

7   Once the meat ball are cooked, remove from heat, garnish with fresh coriander leaves and serve.

Minced Meat Ball Curry

Pork Vindaloo

A family favourite, quite hot and spicy but delicious. Served with rice or chapattis.

15 minutes to prepare, 40 minutes cooking time

Serves 4-6

Ingredients

500g pork

4 tbsp oil

1 medium onion, finely chopped

1 inch of fresh ginger clean and cut into
    4 pieces

1 tsp ginger paste *(In addition)*

3 cloves of fresh garlic, cleaned and cut into
    halves

2 tsp garlic paste *(In addition)*

2 green chillies, slit lengthwise

1 tbsp vinegar

1 tsp chilli powder

2 tsp ground cumin

¼ tsp ground turmeric

200g canned tomatoes

2 tsp salt

Method

1   Wash the pork and cut into one inch cubes including lard.

2   Heat oil in a medium size saucepan or pressure cooker.

3   Put the onions and fry until golden brown.

4   Add ginger, garlic, green chillies and vinegar.

5   Add the chilli powder, cumin and turmeric.

6   Add tomatoes and stir well.

7   Add the pork, salt, 250ml of water if using pressure cooker, otherwise, double the quantity of
water and cook until done.

Pork Vindaloo

Cook's Tip

You can thicken the gravy by adding 1 tsp white rice flour and cook until the gravy thickens.

ANGLO-INDIAN COOKERY

Sundries

In this section I have chosen to showcase the most common traditional main course rice dishes. Complimented by recipes like devil chutney and minced meat cutlet

Biryani is a great one-pot rice dish ideal for dinner parties. It can be made with chicken, meat, vegetables and seafood.

The combination of coconut rice, minced meat ball curry and devil chutney are amongst the most popular dishes served to entertain guest at dinner parties by Anglo-Indian families. Minced meat cutlet is another great dish catered for special occasions.

Coconut Rice

A traditional rice dish commonly accompanied with minced meat ball curry and devil chutney.

20 minutes to prepare, 25-30 minutes cooking time

Serves 4-6

Ingredients

2 cups white basmati rice

50g butter

1 tsp salt

2 small pieces of cinnamon

6 cloves

8 green cardamoms

½ tsp turmeric powder

2 cups water

400ml of coconut milk

Garnish

50g cashew nuts (halves). Fry for a minute and keep aside

50g raisins. Fry for minute and keep aside

1 medium size onions sliced, fried golden brown and keep aside

Method

1 In a large non-stick saucepan, heat butter.

2 Add the rice, salt, cinnamon, cloves, cardamoms, turmeric, water, coconut milk and stir.

3 Bring to boil on medium heat, until liquid has evaporated.

4 Cover and cook on low heat until the rice grains are cooked

5 Garnish with cashew nuts, raisins, fried onions.

ANGLO-INDIAN COOKERY

Coconut Rice

Devil Chutney

Mild spicy sauce side dish often served alongside Coconut Rice.

20 minutes to prepare

Serves 4-6

Ingredients

2 dry red chillies (de-seeded)

2 medium size onions chopped fine

2 tbsp raisins

½ tsp chilli powder

1 tsp sugar

2 tbsp vinegar

A pinch of salt

1 tbsp boiled water

Method

1   Grind all the above ingredients to smooth paste.

Cook's Tip

If preferred you can add more sugar or vinegar to get the right consistency and taste.

Lamb Biryani

A rice dish made with spices and lamb. Great tasting and delectable dish that you will enjoy eating.

35 minutes to prepare, 40 minutes cooking time

Serves 4-6

Ingredients for cooking the lamb

500g lamb with bone

1 tsp fresh ginger root, crushed

1 tsp fresh garlic, crushed

2 pieces of 1 inch (2.5 cm) cinnamon sticks

3 cloves

3 green cardamoms

¼ tsp turmeric powder

125ml yogurt

1 tsp salt

Ingredients for cooking the rice

2 cups basmati rice (wash and soak for 20 minutes)

3 tbsp oil

2 onions, finely sliced

4 pieces of 1 inch (2.5 cm) cinnamon sticks

6 cloves

6 green cardamoms

2 bay leaves

1 star anise (optional)

2 black cardamom (optional)

1 tsp fresh ginger root, crushed

2 tsp fresh garlic, crushed

4 green chillies, slit

4 tsp green coriander, chopped

4 tsp mint leaves, chopped

Method

1 Add the ingredients for cooking the lamb except the yogurt, two cups of water in a large saucepan or pressure cooker and cook until tender.

2 Separate the broth from the lamb and keep aside for cooking the rice. Mix the yogurt with the cooked lamb and set aside.

3 Heat oil in a non-stick or heavy-base saucepan add the sliced onions, cinnamon, cloves, green cardamoms, bay leaves, star anise, black cardamoms and fry until the onions are golden brown. Add ginger, garlic, green chillies and fry for 2 minutes.

4 Add the saved broth and water to make 4 cups in total, bring to a boil.

5 Now add the soaked rice and cook for 8 minutes uncovered. Add the lamb with the yogurt, coriander leaves, mint leaves and mix well. Simmer on very low heat for 8-10 minutes. Sever hot.

Lamb Biryani

Cook's Tip

Similar recipe can be used for making chicken biryani.

Minced Meat Cutlet

Spiced minced lamb covered with potatoes mash. Makes a grand accompaniment to a main dish.

15 minutes to prepare, 35-40 minutes cooking time

Serves 4-6

Ingredients

500g lean minced lamb

5 tbsp oil

1 medium onion, finely chopped

2 green chillies minced

1 tsp ground black pepper

¼ tsp ground turmeric

2 tbsp tomato puree

1 ½ tsp salt

1 inch of fresh ginger, cleaned and minced

½ tsp ground cinnamon

¼ tsp ground clove

2 tbsp roughly chopped coriander leaves

3 potatoes, boiled and mashed

25g butter

50 g bread crumbs

3 eggs, beaten

Oil for frying

Method

1   Heat the oil in a medium size saucepan.

2   Put the onions, green chillies and fry until golden brown.

3   Put the pepper, turmeric, Tomato puree and stir.

4   Immediately put minced meat, 1 tsp salt and stir well until the meat has blended with the masala.

5   Now put ginger, cinnamon, clove, coriander leaves and one cup (250ml) water. Cover and cook for 10 minutes on medium heat or until done.

6   Mix with the mashed potatoes, butter, ½ tsp salt and set aside.

7   To make one cutlet, sprinkle some bread crumbs on a clean surface, lay a ball of mashed potatoes and flatten gently. Now add two or three tsp of mince and cover with mash. Ensure that the mash is coated well with bread crumbs

8 Now gently dip the cutlet in the egg and fry with oil in a shallow frying pan. This will give the cutlet a smooth finish.

Minced Meat Cutlet

Cook's Tip

As an alternative, you could dip the mash in egg first and then bread crumbs for a rough finish.

Plain Basmati Rice

Basmati rice has a fragrance that make this rice dish tasty without added spices.

20 minutes to prepare, 15 minutes cooking time

Serves 4

Ingredients

200g white basmati rice

1 tbsp oil

½ tsp salt

400ml boiling water

Method

1 Soak the rice in sufficient water for 15 minutes. Then drain the water and keep aside.

2 In a medium size saucepan place the rice, oil, salt and boiling water.

3 Cover and allow it to simmer on low heat for 11 minutes.

4 Now remove the cover and stir gently, sampling a few rice grains to check if it has cooked. All the water should have been absorbed.

5 Remove from heat. Fluff up the rice with a fork or spoon before serving.

Cook's Tip

Alternatively, you can boil 1 litre of water, when the water has reached boiling point, lower the heat, drop in the rice grains and stir. Now add salt to taste. Cook on low heat for about 12 minutes. Remove from heat and stain the cooked rice using a colander.

Deserts

In this section I have included many of the family favourite sweets made during Christmas season. They are all amazing and delicious sweets. Whichever one you choose to try out, you will not be disappointed. They are really easy to make.

Dhol Dhol and Kul Kuls are guaranteed to be prepared by many Anglo-Indian families during the Christmas season to offer to guest.

Christmas Cake

A celebration rich fruit cake with icing

Ingredients

200g raisins

200g currants

200g sultanas

50g mixed whole candied peel, finely chopped

50g glace cherries, finely chopped

200g plain flour

1 tsp mixed spice

A pinch of salt

200g unsalted butter

200g light soft brown sugar

4 eggs, lightly beaten

2 tsp finely grated orange rind

¼ cup orange juice

50g coarse almonds

¼ cup brandy

Icing as desired

Method

1 Mix the dried fruit, peel and cherries together and set aside

2 Sift plain flour, spice and salt in a large bowl. Mix well and keep aside

3 Beat the butter and sugar in small mixing bowl until light and creamy. Add eggs gradually, beating thoroughly. Add the orange rind, orange juice and continue beating until they blended well.

3 Empty the mixtures into a large bowl including the fruits mixture. Add almonds and brandy. Stir until the mixture is almost smooth.

4 Put the mixture into a 20 cm round tin lined with greaseproof paper.

5 Bake in a cool oven (gas mark 2) on lower shelf of the oven for 3 ½ to 4 hours or until the skewer comes out clean when inserted in the centre of the cake. Allow it to cool for 15 minutes in the tin before transferring it onto a wire rack.

6 Cover with royal icing or marzipan or left plain as desired.

Christmas Cake

Coconut Sweet

Coconut base sweet, made during Christmas season complimenting other traditional sweets

Ingredients

2 cups desiccated coconut

2 ½ cups sugar

1 cup milk

1 tsp butter

1 tsp vanilla essence

¼ cup of water

½ tsp pink food colour

Method

1 In a heavy-based saucepan, heat the sugar with water over high heat.

2 After the sugar has dissolved, add the coconut, vanilla essence, milk, butter and stir well.

3 Now low the heat and keep stirring the mixture until it thickens.

4 Now add the food colour and continue stirring until the mixture has combined and separates from the sides of the saucepan.

5 Check if the right consistency is reached by spooning a little mixture, cooling and tasting the mixture.

6 Remove from heat and empty the mixture into a greased shallow dish or plate, spread evenly and allow it to cool. Neatly cut them into diamond shapes and serve.

Cook's Tip

For best results, allow the mixture to set overnight in the refrigerator. You can increase the quantity of sugar depending on your taste.

Dhol Dhol

A family favourite made during Christmas season made using a microwave oven.

Ingredients

2 cups of red rice flour (shifted) or
   Red Glutinous rice flour

2 cups of sugar

2 cups of coconut milk

1 tsp of vanilla essence

1 tsp of almond essence

1 tsp of Ghee

Handful of chopped cashew nuts

Method

1 Mix all the ingredients together except the ghee and chopped cashew nuts.

2 Cook in microwave oven for 5 minutes. Do not cover the mixture while cooking.

3 Remove it from the microwave and mix well (preferably using an electric hand mixer)

4 Now add the ghee and chopped cashew nuts and cook in the microwave oven for 7 minutes.

5 Remove from microwave and mix it well with a spoon (do not use electric hand mixer).

6 Return it to the microwave oven and cook for further 5-8 minutes. If you would like it firmer, cook it for a few more minutes.

7 Put the mixture while hot into a greased dish and spread evenly after it cools down cut into cubes.

Cook's Tip

For best results, allow the mixture to set overnight in the refrigerator.

Kul Kuls

A traditional family favourite made during Christmas season. Time consuming process but well worth the effort.

Ingredients

400g plain flour

200g semolina

3 egg yolks

100g butter

A pinch of salt

100g sugar

200ml coconut milk

200ml water for kneading

1 tsp lemon juice

1 tsp baking powder

Oil for deep frying

For sugar coating finish

200g sugar

200ml water

Method

1 Mix the flour, semolina, egg yolk and butter. Add the salt, sugar and coconut milk, water, lemon juice, baking powder and knead into firm dough. Cover and leave the dough to rest for at least an hour.

2 Now make small (marble size) rounds shaped balls from the dough. Flatten each round on to the back of a fork or new comb, pressing gently and rolling at the same time forming ridges on top. Lay the rolled kul kuls on greased paper or plates.

3 Now heat the oil and when the oil is really hot, drop few kul kuls at a time, ensuring they do not stick to each other. Fry on low heat until lightly brown on all sides.

4 Remove the kul kuls few at a time, draining the oil and transferring them onto a paper kitchen towel.

ANGLO-INDIAN COOKERY

For sugar coating finishing

1 In a medium size saucepan mix sugar, water and heat stirring frequently.
2 Cook until the syrup thicken to the right consistency (when a blob of syrup dropped in cold water hardens)
3 Drop the kul kuls few at a time into the syrup, mix and coat evenly.
4 Allow the sugar coating to dry up before serving.

Cook's Tip

You can store them in an airtight container for couple of weeks and consume them as and when required.

Milk Sweet

A simple sweet made with milk powder using microwave oven.

Ingredients

300g Milk powder

200g caster sugar

2 tbsp water

1 tsp vanilla essence

25g butter

Method

1   Mix in a medium size microwave bowl the milk powder, caster sugar, water and stir.

2   Cook in microwave on medium high for 5 minutes.

3   Take it out, add the vanilla essence and stir.

4   Return to microwave for another 3 ½ minutes.

5   Remove and spread onto lightly buttered dish to cool.

6   Cut into diamond shapes.

Rose Cookies

A vanilla flavoured flower shaped cookie with fennel seeds

Ingredients

2 cup plain flour

2 cups rice flour

2 medium size eggs, beaten

2 tsp sugar

1 tsp vanilla essence

1 tsp fennel seeds

½ cup coconut milk

Method

1   Mix the above ingredients to a thick batter with coconut milk.

2   Heat oil in a deep frying saucepan.

3   When the oil is hot, dip the rose cookie mould into the batter.

4   Keep it immerse for few seconds until the batter comes off the Mould.

5   Cook until light brown and remove from saucepan.

Christmas Treats

Homemade Wines

Included here are the two of the most popular homemade wines. They are relatively easy to make and store for special occasions like Christmas time.

Ginger Wine

A sweet and mild version of wine often made during Christmas season.

Ingredients

200g fresh ginger root (finely sliced)

4 lemons

1.5 kg sugar

4 liters of water

1 dried red chilli

5g white wine Yeast

Yeast nutrient

Method

1   Peel the ginger and cut into fine slices

2   Zest and juice the lemons and keep aside

3   In a large saucepan, add ginger, sugar, 2 liters of water, dried red chilli, zest of lemon and bring them to boil on low heat.

4   When cooled, empty the boiled contents into a fermenting bucket with additional 2 liters of boiled cooled water.

5   Then add the juice of the lemon, yeast (follow the instructions on the packet) and yeast nutrients.

6   Cover and leave to ferment for four days.

7   Then use a sieve and muslin cloth to strain and squeeze the liquid via a funnel into a demijohn or in sterilised bottles. Ginger wine can, if necessary, be sweetened to taste before serving.

ANGLO-INDIAN COOKERY

Grape Wine

A sweet and mild version of wine often made during Christmas season.

Ingredients

1 Kg dark black grapes

2 litres of water

1 kg sugar

5g red wine yeast

200g fresh black dates

250g apples (optional)

Method

1 Crush the grapes, add sugar, water, black dates, apples, red wine yeast and store them in a jar sealed for 40 days.

2 For the first 21 days open jar and stir it every day.

3 On 41st day strain the mixture using a fine cloth, squeezing out the juice.

4 Taste the wine to ensure it has correct sweetness and strength, if required add more sugar.

5 Wine can be stored in sterilised bottles, loosely sealed with a cork and kept in a cool place. Can be consume as and when required.

Lightning Source UK Ltd.
Milton Keynes UK
UKIC02n1511261115
263556UK00006B/32